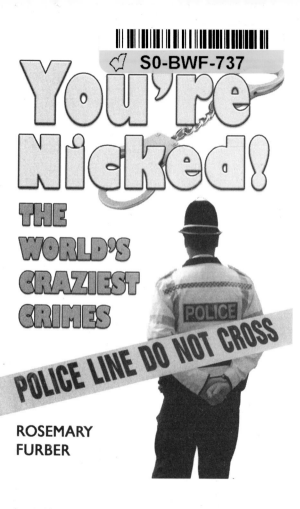

S0-BWF-737

You're Nicked!

THE WORLD'S CRAZIEST CRIMES

POLICE

POLICE LINE DO NOT CROSS

ROSEMARY FURBER

Crombie Jardine
Publishing Limited
Office 2
3 Edgar Buildings
George Street
Bath
BA1 2FJ

www.crombiejardine.com

This edition was first published by
Crombie Jardine Publishing Limited in 2007

Text copyright © Rosemary Furber, 2007

All rights are reserved. No part of this publication may be
reproduced, stored in a retrieval system, or transmitted, in any form
or by any means, electronic, mechanical, photocopying, recording or
otherwise, without the prior written permission of the publisher.

ISBN 978-1-906051-09-9

Written by Rosemary Furber

Typesetting and cover design
by Ben Ottridge

Printed and bound in Great Britain by
William Clowes Ltd, Beccles, Suffolk

CONTENTS

INTRODUCTION

Crime saved my life. When I was a law student, I could have died of boredom if I hadn't discovered the criminal law course. The casebook had a laugh on every page and the big lesson was that if you're going to do something wrong, you might as well enjoy it. Like Robert Boyd, for example, whose excuse for stealing lingerie at sword point was that he thought he was a female elf at the time…

YOU'RE NICKED!

This is a collection of recent daft
crimes featuring dodgy priests,
drunken drivers, idiots, perverts,
pranksters, old and young...

And the moral of it all? If at first you
don't succeed, destroy all the evidence.

Rosemary Furber
2007
www.rosemaryfurber.co.uk

AS BRIGHT AS ALASKA IN DECEMBER

A robber in Grantville, California might have known it wasn't going to be his day when he couldn't see much out of his Ronald Reagan mask. In the bank he got all tangled up in his cape and dropped his gun. Outside, his getaway car got hemmed in by a delivery van. Then a dye bomb exploded in his swag bag ruining all the money. It must have

YOU'RE NICKED!

been the perfect end to a perfect day
when he got arrested.
(Week, 7 October 2006)

Knute Falk (no, really) was all ready
for his first bank robbery. His gun was
loaded, his cash bag was ready and
he had a bandanna over his face. Falk
had just removed $188,655 from the
Bank of America in Beaverton, Oregon
when he realised he'd forgotten one

AS BRIGHT AS ALASKA
IN DECEMBER

important thing. He'd parked his getaway car several blocks away and needed another getaway car to get to it. He asked a customer for his keys – to a car just outside – but Falk couldn't get that car to open. He ripped off his mask, stomped back into the bank for help, and was arrested in minutes.

(foxnews.com, 22 June 2004)

YOU'RE NICKED!

In January 2006 Nick Flynn tripped on his shoelace and fell down the stairs in the Fitzwilliam Museum in Cambridge. He collided with three 17th-century vases which turned out to be worth £500,000. 'I didn't start saving,' Mr Flynn said, 'I knew it wasn't my fault.' Then in April, twenty-five police officers turned up at his home at 7am, some in stab vests, others ready to kick the door in. He spent a night in the police cells. 'It wasn't too heavy,' said Mr Flynn after he was released without charge, 'the police kept offering me tea

AS BRIGHT AS ALASKA
IN DECEMBER

and beans and potato wedges. I felt like
Caravaggio!'
(Guardian, 22 June 2006)

A spliff a day keeps reality away.
Stephen West (20) asked the staff to
take care of his cannabis stash for him
while he was busy in the dock at Wigan
Magistrates' Court. He was arrested
and charged with possession.
(Times, 27 June 2006)

YOU'RE NICKED!

Some people have a brain like Einstein's – dead since 1955. Eloise Reaves (50) crossed a car park in Putnam County, Miami to complain to a policeman about some bad crack cocaine she'd bought. She demanded that he help her get her money back, and was promptly arrested.

(news4jax.com, 18 December 2006)

AS BRIGHT AS ALASKA
IN DECEMBER

What some people lack in intelligence they make up for in stupidity. When Daniel Alexander (18) turned up for a job interview, staff at an Ipswich sports shop were pretty impressed... by his cheek. He'd starred in their CCTV footage the day before when he walked out of the shop with a £28 hooded top, without paying.

(Evening Star, 28 June 2006)

YOU'RE NICKED!

Almadeo Salguero (21) stopped a car at gunpoint, ordered out the three people inside and drove it away along with its stereo system. It wasn't long before the car owner got a call. 'I don't want there to be any hard feelings,' the thief said, 'but how do you hook up your amp?' He'd dumped the car and was trying to get the stereo to work before he flogged it. The owner hung up and when Salguero called again, a police sergeant answered. It didn't take long to track him down and arrest him.

(Security Solutions magazine, issue 29)

AS BRIGHT AS ALASKA
IN DECEMBER

A former policeman from Serbia went into his bank to check his balance, and managed to leave his account card behind. His overdraft must have upset him because he went back with a knife and robbed the branch of around £10,000. He went back a third time, and got arrested trying to deposit the stolen loot in his own account. He also reported the loss of his card.

(Yahoo News, 12 December 2006)

YOU'RE NICKED!

They say television's a medium because so little of it is rare or well done. That didn't stop a thief breaking into a house in Mussidan, France and relieving a pensioner of his television set. But he forgot the remote control, so while the pensioner was out reporting the matter to the police, the thief came back for it. Neighbours called the police, who caught him red-handed.

(Scotsman, 15 November 2006)

AS BRIGHT AS ALASKA
IN DECEMBER

In some prisons it's easy to have a suit for every day of the week; it's an orange jumpsuit and you wear it every day.

Oscar Aponte escaped from prison and thought he'd celebrate by trick-or-treating with his son in Peekskill, north of New York City. Was he congratulating himself on his clever choice of Halloween costume when he felt the hand of the law on his collar? Maybe not… he was wearing his orange prison jumpsuit at the time.

(ABC newsonline, 2 November 2006)

YOU'RE NICKED!

Too bad stupidity isn't painful. Bryan O'Gorman (28) needed someone to help him carry his stolen goods over a fence, and asked an off-duty policeman. *(Times, 15 November 2006)*

Do it yourself? Do it right or they'll do you. Chris Pendery (26) wanted to convert his attic into an extra bedroom, so he sawed through the

AS BRIGHT AS ALASKA
IN DECEMBER

timbers holding up the roof and lined
the floor with chipboard that caved
in the minute anyone stood on it.
'Basically, it's a DIY disaster,' Pendery
said after he admitted causing £15,000
worth of criminal damage to the
housing association house at Leicester
Crown Court.
(Telegraph, 24 April 2004)

YOU'RE NICKED!

Some guys have more brains in their little fingers than they have in their heads. Jared W. Anderson (20) had seen the Jackass movie. He'd also had a few drinks when he pulled down his pants and let Randell D. Peterson (43) spray lighter fluid on his genitals and set him on fire. While he was being treated for second degree burns in the burns unit in St Paul, Minnesota, Andersen begged that nobody get in trouble about the stunt. But his friend's been charged anyway with felony battery and first-degree reckless endangerment and faces up to ten years in prison.
(Chicago Sun-Times, 9 March 2007)

AS BRIGHT AS ALASKA
IN DECEMBER

Mr Fagan accidentally stopped his car on a policeman's foot and refused to budge. Can you commit a crime by not doing something?, Mr Fagan pleaded in court. Surely all he'd done was not drive on, and that's usually a good thing when the police want a word, isn't it? No. Failing to remove the car was part of a continuing act, and his attitude didn't help.

(Fagan v Metropolitan Police commissioner, 1969)

YOU'RE NICKED!

So many botched ATM thefts, so little
time. Let's start with the Latvians who
smashed an Audi through supermarket
doors in Leipaja at 4.30am, knocked
an ATM out of its casing, shoved it on
a trailer and dropped it as they drove
away. And kept driving. 'The possibility
of getting money out of a stolen ATM is
close to zero,' said a spokesman for the
ATM company, 'the money is held in
a metal strongbox inside. If somebody
tries to cut it open, the banknotes burn
up from the heat generated by sawing
through such a thick layer of metal.'
(Yahoo News, 30 August 2007)

AS BRIGHT AS ALASKA
IN DECEMBER

Maybe Independence Day wasn't the best day to try and steal an ATM in Milwaukie, Oregon. First the tie-down straps snapped. When the would-be thieves tried to scoop it up with a 27,000lb front loader, they just pushed it further into the bank and couldn't get to it. The police found the front loader and a dump truck both on fire and the trailer abandoned. Anyone with information about two men running away in a filthy temper, please contact the Milwaukie Police.

(www.courttv.com, 1 July 2006)

YOU'RE NICKED!

Johan Dumon (62), a Belgian antiques dealer, came back from holiday to find that instead of breaking in to his shop, somebody had opened it up and sold £15,000 worth of goods in a two-day sale. Dumon said, 'I can only conclude the burglar was a clever man. Instead of dragging it all out of the house he sold it on the spot.'

(ananova.com, 8 March 2007)

AS BRIGHT AS ALASKA
IN DECEMBER

Mr Pembliton thought he'd settle an
argument by throwing a stone at his
opponents. He missed and broke
a window. He was convicted of
malicious damage to property, and
appealed. He might have been so
annoying that even his food disagreed
with him, but he knew his criminal law.
To be guilty of a crime, you have to
mean it as well as do it, and he'd meant
to hurt his opponents, not the window.
The court agreed, and he was let off.
(R v Pembliton (1874) LR 2 CCR 119)

YOU'RE NICKED!

Two men have been arrested for filling footballs with cement and leaving them around Berlin. They put signs beside the footballs asking people to kick them, and at least two people tried. They regretted it of course, but not as much as the pranksters who are in the dock for causing serious injury. Who says the Germans have no sense of humour?

(Reuters, 5 July 2006)

WHAT'S LOVE GOT TO DO WITH IT?

Thomas Stepiowski was working in a Dorset factory, and missed his Polish homeland so much, he took to fondling women's breasts and pinching their bottoms while making grunting noises. The 'Polish Borat' claimed this behaviour was normal in Eastern Europe. Weymouth magistrates didn't agree. Neither, incidentally, did his female interpreter. He was jailed for nine months.

(Daily Mail, 8 November 2006)

YOU'RE NICKED!

Meanwhile on the Mumbai sea front, more than 100 couples discovered the price of love when they were arrested for kissing and holding hands. Kissing in public is technically illegal in India. Lovers carted off for being found in 'objectionable positions' faced fines of up to 1,200 rupees (about £14.30).
(Times, 7 April 2007)

WHAT'S LOVE GOT TO DO WITH IT?

Women loved it when Simon Francis Jobson drove them round south east Queensland in a fire engine. They were even more impressed when he stopped at traffic accidents and clambered out to help… until he got five years for impersonating a fire officer, breaking into fire stations, stealing AS$10,000 worth of equipment and making off with the trucks. Jobson threw himself on the court's mercy and missed. He claimed he had a 'burning desire' to overcome a mental disorder – the psychologist said he was just seeking attention.

(couriermail.com.au, 15 October 2006)

YOU'RE NICKED!

Who says Australian men aren't romantic? Wayne Floyd was stopped at Sydney airport with a suspicious bulge in his trousers. He had six eggs from endangered species hidden in his underpants, to 'surprise' his girlfriend. He was fined AS$25,000. Flowers next time, Wayne?

(Sky News, 18 July 2006)

WHAT'S LOVE GOT TO DO WITH IT?

Manuel Martinez is in trouble in Mexico City for sexually harassing Maria de Jesus Flores, a rich woman 50 years his senior. 'He said loved me, that he couldn't live without me,' the 98-year-old widow said wearily, and filed a legal complaint. A man is as old as the woman he feels, and as healthy as her bank account.

(Irish Examiner, 2 March 2007)

YOU'RE NICKED!

Robert Boyd was in the dock at Belfast Crown Court for stealing lingerie from a shop at sword point. The reason, he said, was that he believed he was a female elf at the time. Boyd and his friends were playing a fantasy game and Boyd, dressed in a wig, hat and sunglasses, was 'Beho the Elf'. This is an excuse? He also confessed that he might have blurred the line between fantasy and reality.

(BBC News, 6 March 2007)

WHAT'S LOVE GOT TO DO WITH IT?

How do you spot the man at the beach who uses an inflatable doll? He can't take his eyes off the beach balls. Ronald Dotson (39) of Detroit preferred his ladies without a pulse. He'd been out of prison only seven days when he was arrested in Pontiac, Michigan for 'kidnapping' a female mannequin in a skimpy French maid's outfit. It wasn't his first offence. In 1993 he was found partying in an alley with three shop dummies all in women's underwear.

(Lawyer's Weekly, 19 January 2007)

YOU'RE NICKED!

When you're in a hole, isn't it a good idea to stop digging? In Utah's Washington Terrace, several people spotted a man standing naked by glass doors in their apartment block. Police were called and a 42-year-old man was charged with 11 counts of 'lewdness'. Including flashing at the officers who came to arrest him.

(Associated Press, 10 July 2006)

WHAT'S LOVE GOT TO DO WITH IT?

It's better to have loved and lost than to have paid for it and not liked it. Boston police officer Michael LoPriore took no chances. He used his badge, though he was off duty, to force a 19-year-old prostitute into his car and drive her away for sex. He made it clear he wasn't going to pay. She carried on anyway, and while his mind was elsewhere she stole his badge. When he phoned her to get it back, the FBI was listening in.

(Boston Herald, 27 September 2006)

YOU'RE NICKED!

Luck usually means that when our ship comes in, we're queuing at the bus stop but some Tel Aviv thieves won't forget the day they saw two metal cases on a car seat that looked as if they might hold expensive audio equipment. When they got the cases home and opened them, they found they'd broken into the car of Shelley Pasternak, one of Tel Aviv's most famous sexologists. They had a huge haul of sex toys.

(Lawyers' Weekly, 10 November 2006)

WHAT'S LOVE GOT TO DO WITH IT?

Oscar Wilde said that women were meant to be loved, not understood. Women? What about this guy? A Japanese man in his thirties has been found guilty of sexually harassing a female colleague by forcing her to pluck his beard. Eventually she gave in, and now he has to pay her £2,700 compensation.

(Japan Probe, 28 July 2006)

YOU'RE NICKED!

When Keith Rose and his girlfriend got cosy one evening in the foyer of a Sheffield Lloyds TSB bank, he thought nobody else was around, and he was right. But a CCTV camera caught the action, and the branch manager had a good look the next morning. Mr Rose was convicted of 'outraging public decency' and fined £50. He appealed and won: he hadn't actually outraged public decency since there had been no public there at the time to outrage.

(Times, 10 April 2006)

WHAT'S LOVE GOT TO DO WITH IT?

Marriage can be that first sweet step towards divorce; often it's a leap into poverty too. Especially if you marry Emma Golightly. She persuaded a series of men that she was rich and dying of cancer, and she didn't want to die without being a bride. Golightly, who didn't have cancer at all, used her lovers' credit cards (and her own mother's and grandmother's) to ply the men with gifts who would only spot her ruse when the bills came in. She's doing two years in jail.

(Daily Mail, 3 April 2007)

YOU'RE NICKED!

The dismembered body of Melanie McGuire's husband was found in three suitcases in Chesapeake Bay. The police, who know better than most of us that marriage can be murder, arrested Mrs McGuire. Her computer showed up some revealing searches in the days before he died, like 'how to commit murder', instant poisons, undetectable poisons, and 'fatal digoxin doses'. Did she find what she wanted? Hard to say. Mr McGuire died of bullet wounds that matched a gun Melanie bought two days before he disappeared. She could serve up to 30 years.

(Independent on Sunday, 18 March 2007)

WHAT'S LOVE GOT TO DO WITH IT?

Rosanita Nery dos Santos (52) drugged her husband, stabbed him, hacked his body into over 100 pieces and fried them. Police in Salvador, north east of Sao Paulo, said that maybe black magic was involved, or maybe Mrs dos Santos just wanted the life insurance. She claimed that 'masked assailants' came into her house, killed her husband and forced her to cook him. She's doing 19 years in jail.

(Brazzil magazine, 26 March 2007)

YOU'RE NICKED!

Timothy Shepherd's passion for cooking seemed to be getting a little out of hand when he toiled for 48 hours over two outdoor barbecues not long after his girlfriend Tynesha Stewart left him – so he said – for somebody else. Neighbours watched black smoke pouring from his balcony – human flesh needs exceptionally high temperatures to cremate – and when Shepherd was asked what he was up to, he said he was cooking 'for a wedding'. His cordon noir ended up on a rubbish dump, which was handy for the police. The trial continues.
(Times, 27 March 2007)

HOME IS WHERE YOU HANG YOUR HEAD

Don't try this game at home: Tang Xiaowan (25) liked to tease her husband Li Weidong into carrying out her wishes at the point of a sword. When he refused to cook her dinner because he was late for work, Tang grabbed her sword, put it on Li's chest and it slipped, she says, carving him by mistake. He died from blood loss and she faces a manslaughter charge.

(Shanghai Daily, 20 June 2006)

YOU'RE NICKED!

WC Fields reckoned that children should neither be seen nor heard from – ever again. A Russian woman agreed, and hired a hitman to kill her own 17-year-old son so that she wouldn't have to share her one-room flat in Moscow with him. She'd even handed over 2,100 rubles (about £42) for his trouble when the hitman told the police.

(Reuters, 15 March 2007)

HOME IS WHERE YOU HANG YOUR HEAD

A father has changed his son's name to 'Golden Dragon'. The boy used to be called 'Fined Six Thousand and Five Hundred' after his father was fined 6,500 dong (that's right, worth about 30p) for having too many children.
(Times, 8 August 2006)

YOU'RE NICKED!

Parents can be so embarrassing. Mardin Amin was about to board a flight from Chicago to Turkey with his mother when customs people pulled something suspicious from his hand luggage and asked what it was. Amin was far too embarrassed to admit in front of his mum that it was his penis pump and blurted out, 'It's a bomb!' He's been charged with disorderly conduct.

(Week, 1 September 2006)

HOME IS WHERE YOU HANG YOUR HEAD

Two mothers in Woonsocket, Rhode Island (once a sleepy farming community) are in deep trouble after one drove her 13-year-old daughter to school to fight with a rival schoolgirl. Ana Rivera (44) and Maribel Santiago (34) started brawling too and they've all been charged with disorderly conduct.

(Boston News, 10 January 2007)

YOU'RE NICKED!

When a seven-year-old girl phoned
the police and hung up immediately,
officers in Dodge County, Wisconsin
thought the worst and drove straight
round. But the problem was a card
game. The girl had been playing cards
with her grandfather and wanted to
report him for cheating.
(Yahoo News, 8 March 2007)

HOME IS WHERE YOU HANG YOUR HEAD

A mother in her 20s left her child screaming in a pushchair while she joined in a mugging. She knelt on the chest of a 71-year-old woman while another mugger tried to pull off the woman's rings. They got away with the victim's handbag but not her rings.
(Times, 10 March 2007)

YOU'RE NICKED!

An Italian man decided that his wife wasn't putting enough elbow grease into the housework, so he made her scrub the floors on her knees. He's been convicted of ill treatment by Italy's Cassation Court, which is something of a novelty for the mostly male judges of that court. In the past they've decided that sexual abuse of a teenager is less serious when the girl's not a virgin, a woman wearing tight jeans can't be raped and that an 'isolated and impulsive' pat on a woman's bottom at work is absolutely fine.

(Reuters, 18 July 2006)

HOME IS WHERE YOU HANG YOUR HEAD

A mother's place is always in the wrong but some mothers maybe shouldn't have 'em.

Jessica Durham from Montana was photographed letting her 18-month-old Michala suck on a marijuana bong. Jessie reckoned it improved the toddler's appetite and left her 'mellow', and has been sentenced to two years in prison.

(USA v Durham, 2006)

YOU'RE NICKED!

People who say they sleep like a baby usually don't have one.
Derrick Hardy was looking after his girlfriend's 10-month-old daughter when she developed a high temperature. He put her in the freezer. Her mother came home to find the child with frostbite in among the ice cubes and pizzas. Hardy's own lawyer admitted that his client's 'parenting was not up to snuff'. The court wasn't impressed either and sentenced him to 15 months in jail.
(CBC News, 30 January 2007)

HOME IS WHERE YOU HANG YOUR HEAD

'Do you think the excitement's gone out of our marriage?' 'Let's talk about it in the ad break, dear.'

A 45-year-old man in Aachen, Germany got the surprise of his life when he refused his wife's sexual advances and she called in the police. According to their spokesman, 'the police did not feel able to resolve the dispute.'

(Reuters, 3 August 2006)

YOU'RE NICKED!

If you've got it, flaunt it, but be careful who's watching. Newly weds in Paris are in trouble after they were sprinkled with confetti made of shreds of euro notes. It's a crime to destroy legal tender in France.

(Times, 2 August 2006)

Sometimes divorce just isn't enough. Three years after his divorce, Toby Charnaud set off to collect his son

HOME IS WHERE YOU HANG YOUR HEAD

from his ex-wife and wound up being shot, beaten with clubs, dismembered and barbecued. The pieces of his body were strewn among the Thai tigers in Kaeng Krajan National Park. His wife and three of her relatives are serving life sentences for his murder. Strangely, Toby seems to have foretold his own fate: he'd won first prize in a competition with a tale of man whose wife hires a friend to kill him.

(Daily Mail, 1 August 2006)

YOU'RE NICKED!

Always best to get married in the morning, then if it doesn't work out, you haven't wasted the whole day… Adrienne Samen (19) was ready to share the rest of her life with her 'very nice' Marine Cadet just home from Iraq. Things went fine until the bar closed, when she started yelling obscenities, chucking the wedding cake around and hurling vases across the car park. When she stalked off down the road with her wedding dress over her head, the police were called. She gave them the finger and tried to bite the

HOME IS WHERE YOU HANG YOUR HEAD

officer who charged her with breach of the peace. Her bridal suite was the town jail.

(Fox News, 19 August 2003)

AND HOW OLD ARE YOU, SONNY?

A 79-year-old woman in Barnstaple, Devon opened her door to a group of children, some as young as four, who said they were collecting for charity. Their charity began and ended with themselves – they stole her purse.

(Times, 20 March 2007)

AND HOW OLD ARE YOU, SONNY?

At 95 Edward Wigura had reached an age where his back probably went out more than he did. Three girls followed him home and pushed past him into his flat. While the two older ones held him down, a five-year-old went through his pockets and took £60 off him.

(Sun, 9 February 2007)

YOU'RE NICKED!

Ten-year-old Lewis Green of Barnsley, South Yorkshire has threatened other children with knives, stolen bicycles and been liberal with his obscenities to old people and community support officers. He loves alcohol, cigarettes and cannabis and has already developed the knack of stealing from his own family to fund his tastes. He had three criminal convictions by the time Barnsley council imposed a full ASBO on him, making him the UK's youngest holder of an anti-social behaviour order. After the hearing, he went off for a smoke.

(Telegraph, 13 March 2007)

AND HOW OLD ARE YOU, SONNY?

Nine-year-old Semaj Booker was in his third stolen car in a month, and things weren't going well. Police were after him at 80mph and he was heading for a tree. Next morning (unscathed) he decided he'd had enough of living in Seattle and would head for Texas. He cadged a bus to the airport where he sneaked onto a 1,700-mile flight, saying that he'd lost his boarding pass and that his mom was waiting for him in the departure lounge. She wasn't. She was at home, about to be the proudest mummy alive. She boasted that video games had taught him to drive and

that: 'He just showed me that "Mom,
I'm going to achieve anything I want
to do."' She is considering suing
Southwest Airlines.
*(Fox News, 18 January and Times, 26
January 2007)*

Who says fresh air is good for you?
Four children, one only seven years
old, were trying to bring conkers
down from a horse chestnut tree in

AND HOW OLD ARE YOU, SONNY?

Littlehampton, West Sussex when police stopped and searched them. They mistakenly thought the tree was subject to a preservation order.
(Times, 4 October 2006)

Bus passengers were robbed in a remote village in eastern India, so the police turned up. Their list of suspects included a three-month-old baby. 'How

YOU'RE NICKED!

could our little Praveen be named an
accused?' said his bewildered mother,
Shakila Devi…
(Reuters, 3 November 2006)

Murder is always a mistake and
according to Oscar Wilde, we should
never do anything we can't talk about
over dinner. A Florida shop assistant is
accused of trying to murder Jeremius
Howard (14) because he wouldn't buy

AND HOW OLD ARE YOU, SONNY?

a yo-yo. Jeremius was playing with the yo-yo while his sister chose something to eat. She paid up, and the boy put the toy back, saying he didn't want it because it had been opened. Amar Shreiteh pulled him behind the counter and stabbed him with a butcher's knife. *(local6.com, 11 July 2006)*

First you teach them how to talk. Then you have to teach them how to

YOU'RE NICKED!

shut up. A teacher in Lombardy took
a pair of scissors to the tongue of a
noisy seven-year-old pupil and left him
needing five stitches. A security guard
in a Milan public library chose to make
his point silently by holding a revolver
to the temple of an unruly 11-year-old
boy. 'This was a boy in a library,' his
lawyer said, 'not a masked robber in a
jewellery shop.'
(Times, 1 March 2007)

STUDENTS, HUH, WHAT ARE THEY GOOD FOR?

It was Oxford, the exams were over and life was sweet when Jack Orr-Ewing looked into a window and spotted two friends getting intimate. He took out his phone to film the event. The couple were unaware of the gathering crowd until somebody opened the window wider to get a better view, and the young woman said, 'Oh my god.' The couple didn't

YOU'RE NICKED!

mind – 'They saw the funny side,'
Jack said – but he's been chucked out
of the university for a year. Another
undergraduate Martin Tilbury has been
banned from the college bar and has
to spend two months cleaning library
shelves for circulating the video.
(Daily Mail, 12 October 2006)

STUDENTS, HUH, WHAT ARE THEY GOOD FOR?

Nail down the furniture, the students are coming. A gang of students in Eaton County, Michigan developed a taste for restaurant mascots. They stole an inflatable Shrek from a Burger King and a concrete cow from a farm. They had their eye on a 13-foot fibreglass chicken from Joe's Gizzard City but it was chained down, so they made do with detaching its head with a chainsaw.

(cnn.com, 25 June 2004)

YOU'RE NICKED!

'That money talks, I'll not deny.
I heard it once: it said "Good bye".'
An 18-year-old man in Eggmuehl, south
Germany might easily have had Richard
Armour's poem on his mind as he left
his deposits in front of a cash machine
in the bank. He's been detained for
defecating eight times in the bank's
lobby, always on the same spot.
(Reuters, 6 March 2007)

STUDENTS, HUH, WHAT ARE THEY GOOD FOR?

Add some variety to your sex life – use the other hand. Charles Greaves (19) hid a digital camera in a shampoo bottle in the mixed bathroom of halls at the University of Wales in Bangor. When the images of girls taking showers weren't clear enough for him, he put a sign on the door suggesting they take baths instead. But he didn't get clean away with it; he got a suspended prison sentence of two years instead.

(BBC News Wales, 7 September 2006)

YOU'RE NICKED!

She who laughs last hasn't heard the bad news yet...

Janet Lee (21), a student at Bryn Mawr College, Pennsylvania got a three week prison sentence for trying to smuggle flour-filled condoms onto a plane as a joke. At first the security people were relieved she was only carrying flour and not something illegal. That was the good news. The bad news? They didn't like the joke.

(Reuters, 5 January 2007)

OLD ENOUGH TO KNOW BETTER?

Old is when your wife says 'Let's go upstairs and make love', and you say 'Make up your mind, love, I can't do both'.

Police in Bournemouth, Dorset were cracking down on kerb-crawlers when they found a 95-year-old man getting friendly with one of the girls. Who says the police don't have a heart? They let him off with a reprimand because of his age.

(Yahoo News, 20 September 2006)

YOU'RE NICKED!

Two 73-year-old grandparents, with
no previous criminal records, have
been convicted in Aalst in Belgium for
taking over their grandson's business.
He happened to be a major dealer in
heroin, coke and ecstasy.

(Reuters, 18 October 2006)

OLD ENOUGH TO KNOW BETTER?

Winifred Whelan (80, from Liverpool) woke to find a burglar by her bed with a knife in his hand. She rushed downstairs, whipped out her 14-inch kitchen knife and pointed it at the burglar's belly shouting Crocodile Dundee's immortal words, 'You call that a knife? This is a knife!' Luckily her son intervened and, she said, 'stopped me from doing anything stupid'.

(BBC News, 25 July 2006)

YOU'RE NICKED!

Two elderly, silver-haired ladies, wearing court shoes and sensible overcoats, received police cautions after they stole a student's bag at Sunderland railway station. Why did they hand themselves in? Maybe it was the blizzard of headlines like The Grey Train Robbery, Gran Larceny, Nans on the Run, Artful Codgers and Old Blags. They were also caught on camera.

(Reuters, 16 November 2006)

OLD ENOUGH TO KNOW BETTER?

Old lovers never die, they reach for a shotgun. When Reuben Bettis (68) found out that his ex-lover Irene Williams (60) was seeing someone else, he invited her new man, Derek Hamersley (67), to his allotment in Orsett, Essex and filled his stomach with pellets from a 12-bore shotgun. Both had been living in sheltered housing managed by Irene Williams. Mr Bettis is now living in jail.

(Sun, 9 January 2007)

YOU'RE NICKED!

Bob Monkhouse said he still enjoyed sex at 74 – he lived at 76 so it was no distance.

Zivkica Jankovic (52) got shot in the leg in Leskovac, Serbia when her fiancé Radivoje Sinadinovic (77) decided to teach her new lover a lesson. They'd been happy together until love rival Ljubisa Petkovic (78) started boasting about the size of his pension. 'It went to her head,' said Mr Sinadinovic who went to see him with a gun. He was greeted with an axe.

(sandiego.com, 5 March 2007, and Times, 6 March 2007)

OLD ENOUGH TO
KNOW BETTER?

Patricia Tabram (68) of Humshaugh, Northumberland loves gardening so much she's been sentenced to 250 hours' community service for growing her own grass. She grows cannabis in her wardrobe and uses it in stews, ice cream, brownies and curries which she shares with friends. The police raid her flat regularly: 'They'll ask me, "Is it in the hot chocolate tin, Pat?" and of course there it is, every time.'
(Week, 16 March 2007)

AND THE LORD SAID, YOU'RE NICKED!

Journalist Hubertus Wiendl has been done for something he didn't do; he didn't run fast enough. He spotted three 'artists' stealing water from Pope Benedict's garden hose in Regensburg, Bavaria and filmed them. The three hoped to sell bottles of the 'holy water' on eBay and legged it faster than Mr Wiendl, who's been fined €100…

(Stern, 22 August 2006)

AND THE LORD SAID,
YOU'RE NICKED!

Pound notes are the best religion in the world, according to Brendan Behan. Two Roman Catholic priests, Monsignor John Skehan (79) and Father Francis Guinan (63), are accused of stealing $8.6 million over four decades and investing the money in gambling, drinking, holidays in Las Vegas and the Bahamas, and visits to a Miami racetrack. Skehan (who's on the run) allegedly owns properties all over the world, including a pub in Kilkenny. Guinan was arrested at Palm Beach airport; he's said to have funded schooling for his lover's son.

(palmbeachpost.com, 29 September 2006)

YOU'RE NICKED!

Jurors took the Good Book into the jury room with them during Robert Harlan's trial for the murder of a waitress in Colorado. They wanted to look up the passage about an eye for an eye. Harlan appealed to the US Supreme Court arguing that the Bible was an improper influence. His appeal failed.

(democraticunderground.com, 3 October 2005)

AND THE LORD SAID,
YOU'RE NICKED!

Maybe God isn't dead, He just doesn't want to get involved. A 45-year-old Ukrainian man lowered himself into the lion enclosure at Kiev's zoo shouting, 'God will save me, if he exists.' A lioness wasted no time in making a fatal meal of his carotid artery.

(BBC News, 5 June 2006)

YOU'RE NICKED!

Eric Montanez (21) was arrested for feeding more than 30 in a Florida park. Not pigeons, people. He's a member of Orlando's pressure group Food Not Bombs, and broke a city ordinance against feeding more than 25 homeless people at once. Undercover officers spotted him.

(floridatoday.com, 5 April 2007)

AND THE LORD SAID, YOU'RE NICKED!

Thieves broke the eighth commandment when they stole a pillar listing the Ten Commandments from former missionary, Sharon Bennett. The pillar was three feet square and made of concrete, so they must have wanted it pretty badly. So did owner Sharon Bennett who said, 'I forgive them. I just wish they didn't do it.'

(tennessean.com, 29 June 2006)

YOU'RE NICKED!

A man carrying a Bible went around
Penn Township, Pennsylvania knocking
on doors and tried to break in if
nobody answered. A Bible might stop
a bullet but it didn't stop Stephen
Eric Johnson (25) being arrested for
attempted burglary, trespass and public
drunkenness.

(eveningsun.com, 16 October 2006)

AND THE LORD SAID,
YOU'RE NICKED!

Steven Worner, known as Awk,
was standing in the middle of the
B4494 road to Newbury, dressed in
white robes with a shrub tied to his
stomach. He was being promoted to
Lord Protector by chief druid Arthur
Pendragon when a car came round the
corner and knocked Arthur down. Auk
and another druid called Dragonrider
denied violent disorder and damage to
a Jaguar.

(Telegraph, 20 May 1997)

YOU'RE NICKED!

Strippers are often used at Chinese
funerals, to encourage attendance
apparently, but this venerable Chinese
practice is under threat. Five people
were arrested during a lively striptease
for 200 in Beijing. It's what they would
have wanted.

(Reuters, 24 August 2006)

AND THE LORD SAID,
YOU'RE NICKED!

Joe Fish (20) was charged with 'criminal mischief' in Canton, New York after he broke into a funeral parlour and fell asleep. The director's wife spotted knees sticking out of one of the coffins.

When Joyce Sutton's husband died, it was her clairvoyant Paul Williams (48) of Stourbridge, West Midlands who collected her from the hospital. He also had the foresight to steal her cheque

YOU'RE NICKED!

book. They'd met when Mrs Sutton asked him to exorcise the ghost of her husband's first wife from her home. It wasn't long before the psychic had a vision of Mrs Sutton's dead husband telling him that a will was hidden in the grandfather clock. Sure enough, a will forged by Mr Williams turned up in the clock leaving half the estate to Mr Williams. The judge said, 'I am sure you have foreseen that you are going to prison.'

(Times, 13 April 2006)

AND THE LORD SAID,
YOU'RE NICKED!

Charles Rose (35), boss of the Sparkle cleaning company, must have been clean out of his mind when he was caught on CCTV one night running around an East Lothian graveyard, hurdling gravestones and walls without his trousers or underwear. A charge of rubbing his private parts against a headstone was dropped.

(Daily Record, 18 October 2006)

FETCH THE FUR-LINED HANDCUFFS

Marlon Brown (23) might have got away with stealing a monkey (usually £500) if he hadn't been spotted playing with a real monkey in a Clapham park. Marlon claimed that Spongebob, a Bolivian squirrel monkey, could have sneaked into his bag at Chessington World of Adventures. But Mr Brown's DNA was found inside Spongebob's cage. Mr Brown's got a cage of his own now, as a guest of Her Majesty.

(BBC News, 22 March 2007)

FETCH THE FUR-LINED HANDCUFFS

Tristan Maidment (23) met his match when he broke into a Wiltshire pet shop and tried to steal a parrot. Micky, a 50-year-old macaw with a famous temper, bit Mr Maidment so severely that his blood left at the crime scene was enough to convict him. Micky remains as free as a bird.

(BBC News Somerset, 20 July 2006)

YOU'RE NICKED!

Accidents will happen, especially if you're insured. Barney the Doberman wouldn't have been anywhere near the teddy bear display in Wookey Hole Caves, Somerset if the insurance company hadn't insisted on protection for the exhibits. But Barney took it into his doggy head to find out what the bears were made of. In just 15 minutes off the leash, he ripped the guts out of over 100 exhibits, including Elvis Presley's 1909 teddy Mabel. All of this put Barney firmly in the doghouse.

(Times, 3 August 2006)

FETCH THE FUR-LINED HANDCUFFS

In Hohhot, Inner Mongolia, Ms Li's dog liked to laze on the steering wheel while she was driving. It occurred to her to let him control the steering while she worked the pedals. They crashed. She paid. What, had the dog left his wallet at home?

(breitbart.com, 28 August 2006)

YOU'RE NICKED!

Jill Knispel (35) loved to take her work home with her. She worked for Baby Exotic Birds of Englewood, Florida, and managed to smuggle a Greenwing parrot (worth $2,000) home inside her bra. She was caught trying to swap the bird for a vintage car. But the car owner was a friend of her boss... who reckoned that a bird in her bra was worth calling the police for.

(United Press International, 8 November 2005)

FETCH THE FUR-LINED HANDCUFFS

Some people just won't be told; they're the guys who have to pee on the electric rail for themselves. 'Alligators eat small mammals' said the sign in Colwyn Bay zoo in Wales. So Damien French (20) grabbed a rabbit from the children's area and chucked it into the alligator pool, where a large alligator called Albert ate it. Mr French also discovered what his local magistrates are for.

(Guardian, 5 April 2006)

YOU'RE NICKED!

Apparently there are 3,000 spiders on earth for every human being. Mahlon Hector (22) must have reckoned it was time his boss got some of her share; the day before left his job at Marks & Spencer in Leicester, he sent her a Mexican red-kneed tarantula. She got nightmares. Mahlon got 200 hours' community service.

(Telegraph, 7 July 2006)

FETCH THE FUR-LINED HANDCUFFS

What's fifty feet long and lives on
potatoes?
A Russian meat queue.
Border guards in Kazakstan have found
a criminal gang smuggling 14 camels
into Russia.
(Times, 9 February 2007)

Maybe Callum Myers (18) was testing
the nine-lives theory when he dangled
much-loved Tigger the cat over the

YOU'RE NICKED!

open jaws of his Staffordshire bull terrier Gypsy. Gypsy ate the cat. Mr Myers got four months bird.
(Sun, 21 November 2006)

The cat's in the tumble drier, send for a spin doctor!
While Diane Hannon's boyfriend was on holiday, she put his cat in the tumble drier where poor Paws died of a heart attack and scalding. Ms Hannon is banned from owning animals for life.
(Reuters, 5 February 2007)

FETCH THE FUR-LINED HANDCUFFS

Zhang Xinyan (35) had had a few beers at Beijing zoo. After an invigorating nap, he was so overcome by longing to hug a panda that he hurdled over a waist-high railing and got friendly. Gu Gu, a six-year-old male panda, responded by biting him in both legs. Mr Zhang bit back. He got a mouthful of thick fur, and a visit to hospital.

(BBC News, 20 September 2006)

YOU'RE NICKED!

Animal expert Desmond Morris says that if something bites you, it's probably female. Donald Irvin and his crew were burgling a flat in Lancaster, California when Roxy, a two-year-old Chihuahua, valiantly yapped the place down and attacked their ankles. They dumped her in the freezer, where her owner found her shivering but OK.
(NBC4.TV/news, 1 February 2007)

FETCH THE FUR-LINED HANDCUFFS

Colin Hill has been fined for owning a cockerel in the countryside. His pedigree White Sussex, Leo, is regularly full of the joys at three in the morning and crows his little heart out to prove it. Mr Hill, a former gamekeeper, has had to pay £175 plus costs after neighbours in Market Harborough complained.

(Scotsman, 13 March 2007)

YOU'RE NICKED!

Give a man a fish and he'll eat for a day. Teach him how to fish, and he'll sit in a boat and drink beer all day. Give him a gun...
A man robbed a fish farm at gunpoint in Hawkhurst, Kent, and escaped on his bicycle. The staff were so shocked, they couldn't move.
(Times, 12 April 2007)

FETCH THE FUR-LINED HANDCUFFS

'Son, when you participate in sporting events,' said that American sage Homer Simpson, 'it's not whether you win or lose, it's how drunk you get.' A bull-running festival in Tamil Nadu, south India offers the chance to try and grab bulls by their horns as they run by. Not something a sane man would do sober, so a local concoction called arrack has traditionally helped things along. But injuries were slashed from 400 to about 60 when authorities decided to breathalyse participants, animal and human. Seven bulls were disqualified for being drunk.

(Reuters, 18 January 2007)

DON'T VOTE, IT ONLY ENCOURAGES THEM

What's on a drunk's lips is often in the sober man's heart, and should stay there. Wilfred Nkabeka, a 27-year-old estate agent, was sentenced to two years in prison in Zambia for calling President Chiluba 'chikala'. Most newspapers lacked the cojones to translate this as 'a private part'; they said he called the president 'stupid'.

(BBC News, 31 October 2001)

DON'T VOTE, IT ONLY ENCOURAGES THEM

Noel Coward loved criticism of his work, as long as it was unqualified praise.

Turkish journalist Ipek Calislar's biography of the wife of Mustafa Kemal Ataturk had nine print runs in two months. People loved it, especially the story about Turkey's founding father escaping an assassination attempt by dressing in a woman's chador. But it landed Mrs Calislar in court. Had she insulted Ataturk's memory? Fortunately the court reckoned no, the disguise actually made him look good.

(Times, 5 September 2006 and www. englishpen.org, 21 December 2006)

YOU'RE NICKED!

It only seemed like a crime, perhaps, in the boy's mind…
Field Marshall Montgomery gave a schoolboy a lift home once, and asked the lad if he knew who he was. 'It's something to do with "field",' he said as a clue. The boy was impressed. 'What do you do in fields?' he asked. Monty replied, 'I kill people.' The boy asked quietly to be let out of the car.
(Times, 13 October 2006)

DON'T VOTE, IT ONLY ENCOURAGES THEM

War can be like German opera, too long and too loud, but not where the Swiss are concerned. The Swiss 'invaded' Lichtenstein by mistake one night when a company of 170 infantry soldiers wandered about a mile across an unmarked border, realised their mistake and went home again. Nobody in Lichtenstein seems to have noticed.

(Blick, 2 March 2007)

YOU'RE NICKED!

Sometimes it's time to bury the hatchet, between the other guy's ears. On the Ballymurphy estate in Belfast, a long-running dispute has culminated (for now) in a stolen digger charging uninvited into a house at 6am. Luckily nobody was home at the time.

(Times, 7 April 2007)

DON'T VOTE, IT ONLY ENCOURAGES THEM

When Hubert Hoffman (45) was stopped by Warsaw police in a routine check, he went into one about how the country was turning into a dictatorship under President Lech Kaczynski. Officers suggested he show more respect. Mr Hoffman farted, and was promptly arrested.

(Week, 7 October 2006)

I DO OWN THE ROAD

A traffic warden in Rio de Janeiro has confessed to sawing a woman in half after she ignored his advice about where she could park her car. 'Only the bottom part of the corpse has been found,' said police, referring to businesswoman Edna Souza (51).

(Scotsman, 31 August 2006)

I DO OWN THE ROAD

Charlie Macias (39) used his builder's saw to detach a clamp that had been put on his car within the three minutes he'd been in a bank. He got off with a caution. He should have got a round of applause.

(Times, 5 July 2006)

'What gear were you in at the time of the theft, madam?'
'Jeans and a t-shirt, I think, officer.'
A woman in south Sydney dragged a

YOU'RE NICKED!

49-year-old woman out of her car and would have hijacked it if she'd known how to drive a manual car. She couldn't even get into first gear.

(Sydney Morning Herald, 18 October 2006)

There's a set of double yellow lines in Blackburn exactly one metre long. How are they going to enforce that as a no-parking area? Colin Rigby, a Blackburn councillor, said, 'The

I DO OWN THE ROAD

only thing you could park there is a
unicycle.'
(Times, 23 March 2007)

When you've got to go, you've got
to go. In Rudolstadt, East Germany a
driver was only obeying orders when
his satnav said, 'Turn right now!' So he
did, straight into a portable toilet hut
on the roadside. His proper turning
was about 30 yards further on. He did

YOU'RE NICKED!

€2,000 of damage to the hut, and was fined €35.

(Deutsche Welle, 23 October 2006)

On Christmas Day a thief in Redditch broke into a Volvo with a load of presents on the back seat. He was driving away when he checked the rear view mirror and noticed a little old woman sitting among them. The thief showed his goodwill by dragging her

out and dumping her on the pavement.
Luckily she wasn't seriously hurt.
(Yahoo News, 28 December 2006)

Constantino Garcia (43) was happy
to admit he was doing 162mph in a
£100,000 Audi. In fact he was proud of
it. He'd been on an empty motorway
in perfect conditions and said, 'I'm sure
90 percent of people would have done
the same.' The Burgos court agreed.

YOU'RE NICKED!

Mr Garcia's driving had not endangered anyone.

(Reuters, 23 March 2007)

The man handed over £20 and went behind an electricity substation in Boscombe, Dorset, pushing his bike. Lesley Cole (25) followed, and soon they were so busy expressing their appreciation for each other that the police arrested them. The man got off a kerb crawling charge because he'd brought his bike, not a car. Lesley was jailed for ten weeks.

(Cycling Plus, 21 March 2007)

James Yates (46), an American Airlines pilot, had been on a seven-hour drinking session the night before he pitched up to take control of a Boeing 767. He was nearly eight times over the legal limit for the job. His defence was sleep-drinking: that he'd downed a third of a bottle of Bushmills Irish whiskey in his sleep. The jury at Manchester Crown Court took only 90 minutes to acquit.

(Times, 22 March 2007)

Sometimes the horse is so slow, the jockey can die of thirst. Not in Geseke, Germany where faithful Hendrik the horse carried his owner on a pub crawl. In each hostelry the rider would

I DO OWN THE ROAD

ask for 'One for the road, and an apple
for Hendrik' and fire his cap gun.
He was arrested for being drunk on
horseback.
(DNA India, 18 September 2006)

COURT IN THE ACT

Sometimes death is nature's way of telling you to slow down. Former human rights lawyer and judge Marcus Einfeld was caught speeding in Sydney and would have got away with a small fine if he hadn't tried to blame it on somebody else. Pity he chose a woman who'd died three years earlier. He faces jail.

(Australian, 25 August 2006)

COURT IN THE ACT

Ex-policeman Mark Cutherbertson
(49) reckoned he could get out of
a speeding fine in Derbyshire by
pretending to be French. That way,
he'd be less likely to be prosecuted.
But he was caught on camera.
Fromage!
(BBC News, 14 March 2007)

YOU'RE NICKED!

Blackwood magistrates' court in South
Wales is closing after 100 years for
attracting too many criminals. Local
villains got so fond of the place, they
started using it as a club. One group
of girls brought a crate of booze and
merrily lined up the drinks before going
into court. 'It made a farce of the law,'
said a local policeman.
(Times, 7 April 2007)

COURT IN THE ACT

Father Christmas, a judge with a heart and a drunk are all in a bar when they spot a £50 note on the floor. Who gets it? The drunk – the others are fictional characters, aren't they?

Daniel Hardman (21) turned out not to be such a hard man after all when he burst into tears in Liverpool Crown Court. Judge Denis Clark had just sentenced him to six months in jail for chucking a glass at a pub landlord. But when the judge saw Hardman's tears he relented, and suspended his sentence.

(BBC News, 6 July 2006)

YOU'RE NICKED!

Get them by the ball games and their
hearts and minds will follow.
Mid-Kent police invited suspects to
hand themselves in. If they didn't, the
police would pay them a visit during
the World Cup games. Custody suites
don't have televisions and the guys
would miss the soccer. Seventeen
villains turned themselves in.
(Times, 26 June 2006)

COURT IN THE ACT

Somebody stole a motorbike worth £1,200. Its 18-year-old owner complained to Avon and Somerset police, who told him that they had to let the thief go free. They knew exactly who he was but he had no helmet, which meant that if he fell off and was hurt, he could sue the police. For health and safety reasons most forces follow a similar policy.

(Times, 30 June 2006)

YOU'RE NICKED!

Is it theft or is it recycling? Jon Eipp
felt pretty green when he was
caught wheeling six court computers
and monitors out of Marin County
Courthouse in a recycling bin.
(New York Post, 21 September 2006)

Lawyers are boycotting Cheltenham
magistrates' court until they can
have their own lavatories again. One
thousand pounds in fines went missing

COURT IN THE ACT

from a court office, so that whole area of the court had to be locked. This meant that the lawyers had to share public loos with the defendants, which the lawyers say leaves them nothing to go on.

(Times, 5 March 2007)

For Stuart Kennedy (24), it should have been just another day at the office. The music started and he began to peel off

YOU'RE NICKED!

his police uniform piece by piece. Two police officers, both female, watched his strip act all the way to the end, and then charged him with impersonating a police officer and carrying an offensive weapon.

(Times, 27 April 2007)

VILE BODIES

Simon Moran (38) had used the M65 as his 'corridor of crime' for years and thought he'd got away with burglary again, no sweat. Until he wiped his forehead on a victim's glove and left it behind. The sweat led Bolton police to his DNA sample, and led him to four years in prison for six burglaries. Similar offences were taken into consideration – 108 of them.

(Bolton News, 5 October 2006)

YOU'RE NICKED!

Dr Egidius Panis, a senior medical health officer at Heathrow, set off looking like a cyberman in goggles, overalls and overshoes to examine a passenger with suspected SARS. The General Medical Council, who weren't such Doctor Who fans, struck him off with immediate effect for unduly alarming other passengers.

(Aviation Today, 12 March 2007)

VILE BODIES

Mohammad Kashif needed an
operation to remove his gall bladder.
After four and a half hours' surgery
in Karachi by Dr Syed Kashif Mateen,
Mr Kashif woke and was duly shown
a severed gall bladder complete with
stones. Days later Mr Kashif was
still feeling poorly. A second opinion
discovered that his own gall bladder
was still inside him, but his right kidney
wasn't. The going rate for a healthy
human kidney is US$18,000.

(PakTribune, 12 July 2006)

YOU'RE NICKED!

Ismail Canseven (73) has been
sentenced in Kutahya, Turkey to a
26-day reading and writing course
at his local library because he didn't
vote on time in his village election. Mr
Canseven is blind. 'What am I going to
do in a library?' he said, 'I can't see out
of either of my eyes, and I can't read or
write anyway.'
*(Librarian and Information Science News, 6
December 2006)*

VILE BODIES

Omed Aziz didn't see the police coming when they asked him to wind down the windscreen and take off his sunglasses. Mr Aziz lost his sight in a bomb blast in Iraq and has become the first blind person to be done for dangerous driving. His friend, who'd already been banned from driving, was guiding him from the passenger seat. They'd reached 35mph and negotiated two traffic islands and a corner in Oldbury, West Midlands before they were stopped.

(Times, 5 September 2006)

SOMETHING YOU ATE?

WC Fields loved cooking with wine so much, he even put some in the food. Bad idea. A flaming chorizo was already alight at a North Kensington restaurant when the waiter decided it could do with a splash more rum. Flames erupted over a customer 'as if someone had put a flame-thrower to her face'. The restaurant owner was fined £4,000.

(Sun, 13 April 2007)

SOMETHING YOU ATE?

Kids used to bring an apple for the teacher. Now it's cookies laced with laxative. Julie Hunt's daughter got low marks at school in Anson, Maine so she thought it was time to teach the teacher a lesson. Julie and her daughter baked cookies together, crushed a whole box of laxative pills into them and left them for the teacher with a note saying, 'Hope you enjoy them'. The teacher shared them around the whole class and four children fell ill. Mom was arrested for assault.

(BBC News, 10 May 2006)

YOU'RE NICKED!

Eric de Jersey (61) told a Guernsey court that the flesh-coloured item poking out from under his newspaper was a jumbo frankfurter. He was found guilty of indecent exposure.
(Week, 29 October 2006)

Two men in Itzehoe, north Germany broke into a supermarket and stole... one cake.
(Times, 30 August 2006)

SOMETHING YOU ATE?

Inmates from La Moye prison, Jersey were outraged when their prize leeks weighing about 8lb each were stolen from the Royal Horticultural Show in Malvern.

(Times, 28 September 2006)

You can take the guy out of the trailer but you can't take the trailer out of the guy. Gerrard O'Leary and his gang of Irish travellers broke into a Russian

YOU'RE NICKED!

millionaire's home in Harrow, stole £2 million in cash, jewellery and sports cars – it was London's biggest ever burglary – and celebrated with a meal at McDonald's and a shopping trip to Primark.

(Times, 4 August 2006)

SOMETHING YOU ATE?

Customs officers at Coventry airport found £30,000 worth of cocaine hidden inside more than 140 prunes. The smugglers are on the run.
(Yahoo News, 6 February 2007)

A Tokyo robber calmly ate noodles and fried chicken in an Osaka noodle bar before he produced a knife and demanded all the takings. He then rolled off a 1000 yen bill and paid for

YOU'RE NICKED!

his meal. He even waited for 100 yen change before he legged it.

(Reuters, 2 November 2006)

How to be a real cool lover? Kenneth George Bilwin II (28) was caught trying to sneak three bags of frozen shrimp into his pants in a Giant Food Store in West York, Pennsylvania.

(York Daily Record, 12 October 2006)

SOMETHING YOU ATE?

Madison police have arrested a 53-year-old man for stealing oil, sugar, eggs, flour and a delivery truck. Sweet.
(gazetteextra.com, 9 October 2006)

King of the foodie criminals must be Armin Meiwes, the German cannibal who met his victim, Bernd Brandes, through the internet. Meiwes had longed to be a cannibal ever since he was a boy; he'd even fantasised

YOU'RE NICKED!

about eating Sandy, the boy in Flipper. Brandes' fantasies ran to pretty extreme masochism, so it seemed to be a marriage made in internet heaven. In his timbered farmhouse in Rotenburg, Meiwes first cut off Brandes' penis and cooked it. Both men tried to eat it, but couldn't manage it all. At this point Brandes became somewhat distressed and set about killing himself with sleeping pills while Meiwes read a Star Trek novel. Meiwes says he then cooked up to 20kg of his victim with garlic, pepper,

SOMETHING YOU ATE?

nutmeg and a bottle of South African red, and ate it. He's serving eight and a half years for manslaughter.

(Guardian, 31 January 2004)

THANK GOODNESS FOR GOODNESS

Mae West said she liked two things hard and one of them was eggs. The other probably wasn't moral decisions. A bustard's egg, wrapped in bubblepack and nestling in a tin, turned up at the Overbecks Museum in Salcombe, Devon accompanied by a note. The egg had been stolen from the museum 43 years earlier. The note said, 'I do apologise profusely.'
(Week, 21 October 2006)

THANK GOODNESS
FOR GOODNESS

Pan Aiying, a teacher from Shandong, had her bag stolen. She minded losing cards and cash, but what she really missed was her phone so she kept texting the thief. After 21 texts, the thief returned her bag and phone with a note saying, 'You are so tolerant even though I stole from you. I'll correct my ways and be an upright person.'

(Reuters, 22 January 2007)

YOU'RE NICKED!

King Mohammed VI of Morocco has hit on a great way to solve prison overcrowding. He celebrated his daughter's birth by releasing nearly 9,000 prisoners from jail. He reduced sentences of another 24,000 and commuted 11 death sentences.
(netscape.com, 3 March 2007)

THANK GOODNESS
FOR GOODNESS

Algeria's biggest private company, the Khalifa Group, collapsed and Abdelmoumen Khalifa was tried in connection with a $1 billion fraud. He was sentenced – in absentia – to life imprisonment. He's doing his best to serve his sentence in absentia too.

(Times, 23 March 2007)

YOU'RE NICKED!

After 53 years in jail in Aachen, Hubert Niemann (71) has been offered a place in an open prison, and has said no thanks, he's happy where he is. There'll be no coming-out party either for a 59-year-old German murderer known as Gerold H; he's spent 34 years behind bars and has refused an offer to be let out.

(Reuters, 21 October 2006 and Times, 3 March 2007)

THANK GOODNESS
FOR GOODNESS

Some people might say that the only
only injustice here was that a New
York cabbie accepted a tip of 30 cents
on a $10.70 fare...

Osman Chowdhury (41) had accepted
the tip when he found that his
passenger had left her bag behind. He
took it to the New York Taxi Workers
Alliance where they looked inside, and
found diamond rings worth $500,000.
Mr Chowdhury tracked down the
owner's apartment, returned the rings,
and reluctantly accepted her offer of

YOU'RE NICKED!

$100 reward to cover the fares he'd
lost while trying to find her.
(BBC News, 9 February 2007)

Dennis and Tamie Leporin bought bikes
for Christmas to ride with their young
son and left them in the front garden
in Pensacola, Florida. When the bikes
vanished, they put a sign out there: 'I
hope U crooks enjoy our bikes U stole
– Merry Xmas.' The next evening they

THANK GOODNESS
FOR GOODNESS

heard a knock at their door and found
an envelope from a stranger with $200
inside and a note: 'For every crook
there are 1,000 good people.'
Thank goodness for goodness.
(CBS News, 28 December 2006)

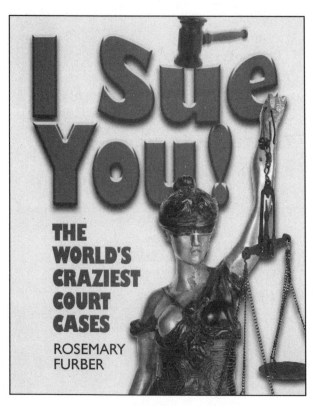

I Sue You!

THE WORLD'S CRAZIEST COURT CASES

ROSEMARY
FURBER

ISBN 978-1-905102-92-1, pb, £4.99

The World's Funniest Puns

Archaeologist: A man whose career lies in ruins.

What's the definition of a will? A dead giveaway.

Did you hear about the butcher who backed into a meat grinder? He got a little behind in his work.

JAMES ALEXANDER

ISBN 978-1-905102-66-2, pb, £4.99

The World's Funniest Laws

JAMES ALEXANDER

In Arizona you can go to prison for 25 years for cutting down a cactus!

Do not say "oh boy" in Jonesborough, Georgia. It's illegal!

On Sundays in Florida, widows must not go parachuting!

It is against the law to take a lion to the cinema in Baltimore!

ISBN 978-1-905102-10-5, pb, £4.99

The World's Funniest Proverbs

JAMES ALEXANDER

Beauty is in the eye of the beer holder

Don't take life too seriously - it's not permanent

Multi-tasking: the art of screwing up everything all at once

Never marry for money; you will borrow cheaper

ISBN 978-1-906051-07-5, hb, £5.99

All Crombie Jardine books are available from High Street Bookshops, Amazon, Littlehampton Book Services, or Bookpost, P.O.Box 29, Douglas, Isle of Man, IM99 1BQ
Tel: 01624 677 237,
email: bookshop@enterprise.net
(postage and packing free within the UK).

If you have enjoyed this book
and have any comments or
suggestions to make, please email:
admin@crombiejardine.com

www.crombiejardine.com

www.rosemaryfurber.co.uk